Glimpse of
DARTMOOR
PONIES

WITHDRAWN

The publishers acknowledge the help of the Dartmoor National Park
and the Dartmoor Pony Society with the publication of this book.

Peninsula
Press

Published by Peninsula Press Ltd
P.O. Box 31
Newton Abbot
Devon TQ12 5XH
Tel: 0803 875875

Printed in Devon by Kingfisher Print & Design, Dartington.

ISBN 1 872640 24 9

*The Dartmoor Pony Society wishes to state that many of the ponies
in the colour photographs of the Drift are of mixed breeding.*

Acknowledgements

The publishers wish to thank the Dartmoor National Park for permission to
reproduce the map on page 39.

Photograph and illustration credits

Dartmoor Pony Society: page 8, by kind permission of Mrs D.Coaker; page 26.
Dartmoor National Park: Front cover, inside front cover; pages 9, 10, 19, 20, 21,
22, 31, 32, inside back cover. **Mr & Mrs P.Taylor:** pages 4, 37. **Mrs Windsor:**
page 5 (top), page 25 (top). **Lucy Hall:** page 5 (bottom), pages 23, 33. **John Lyne:**
page 7. **Mrs D. Coaker:** page 24. **West Country Studies Library:** pages 6, 17, 18,
35. **Lionel Edwards:** page 14 (from *The Maltese Cat* by Rudyard Kipling). **British
Coal Corporation:** page 12. **The National Pony Society:** page 13 (photograph
by Chas White). **Mrs D.Alford:** page 25 (bottom). **Western Morning News &
Evening Herald:** pages 28, 29 (bottom). **Carole Knowles-Pfeiffer:** page 34.
M.V.R. Photographic: page 36. **Mrs V.P.Parkinson:** page 30 (photograph by
Gilsons Photography). **Mrs Jones & Miss Roberts:** page 29 (top) (photograph by
Gilsons Photography).

A
Glimpse of
DARTMOOR
PONIES

WITHDRAWN

Contents

Hisley Pedlar

Introduction

Bellever Newtake

Where did the ponies come from?

The simple answer to this is that nobody knows. For as long as people can remember small hardy ponies have lived on Dartmoor, but the experts tell us that there were none in prehistoric times. Some say they were brought by the Phoenicians in about 1200 BC, when they came trading for tin to the West Country (though footprints found on Shaugh Common have been dated from around 1500 BC) others that tribes such as the Iceni arrived with them already partly domesticated. Certainly they were regularly used when Julius Caesar invaded in 55BC and may well have travelled west to Wales and Devon when the Celts were gradually pushed out of Roman Britain. It is rather nice to think that perhaps a distant ancester of our present-day successful driving ponies once pulled Boadicea's chariot!

Phoenician Ship

Ready for work

There is no doubt whatever that the ponies have played an important part in the lives of the people of Dartmoor. Small but very strong, sure-footed and hardy, energetic but calm, they have adapted to their rugged surroundings, able to withstand the harsh winter conditions, living off gorse and heather as well as the grass and wild herbs, and knowing how to cope with the bogs, the steep valleys and the rocks of the tors. Looking at some of the pampered, stabled ponies of today it is important to remember that the moor is still their natural environment.

To whom do the ponies belong?

Here we are on much safer ground: all the ponies have owners. From earliest times, all over the British Isles, grazing rights have been inherited by certain farms and families living on or near commons. Cattle, sheep and ponies continue to be turned out with their owners' individual brands or other marks. Although living free, most herd animals stay within their own area, known on Dartmoor as a 'leir', apart from young colts driven out to find their own band of mares. For centuries the owners would use certain ponies on the farm or at the mines and then turn them out for breeding. Although few written records were kept, it is pretty certain that stallions were carefully selected to run with the mares, and the Autumn Drifts, when the ponies are brought in for inspection, branding, culling and selling have been going on for centuries.

Autumn Drift

The Fairs, where the selling of stock and the hiring of farm workers and servants took place, have a history of their own. Who knows - Tom Pearce's ill-fated grey mare, who did not survive her overloaded trip to Widecombe Fair and back, may well have been a grey Dartmoor pony! (See *Widecombe Fair*, p.11.)

The farmers living in different parts of the Moor developed their own strains of carefully bred ponies, and the old men used to say they could tell exactly where they were by the type of ponies around them. Human nature being what it is, there is also no doubt that different owners vied with one another to produce the fastest and most beautiful animals, and races and shows not so very different from those we know today were a feature of the life of the Moor.

Huccaby Races 1909

Starting the drift

The road home

Fording the stream

In the yard

Widecombe Fair

'Tom Pearse, Tom Pearse, lend me your gray mare,'
All along, down along, out along, lee.
'For I want to go to Widecombe Fair,
Wi' Bill Brewer, Jan Stewer, Peter Gurney, Peter Davy,
Dan'l Whiddon, Harry Hawk,
Old Uncle Tom Cobley and all.' *Old Uncle Tom Cobley and all.*

'And when shall I see again my gray mare?'
All along, down along, out along, lee.
'By Friday came and Saturday noon,
Wi' Bill Brewer ...'

Then Friday came and Saturday noon,
All along, down along, out along, lee.
But Tom Pearse's old mare hath not trotted home,
Wi' Bill Brewer ...

So Tom Pearse he got up to the top o' the hill,
All along, down along, out along, lee.
And he seed his old mare down a·making her will,
Wi' Bill Brewer...

So Tom Pearse's old mare her took sick and her died,
All along, down along, out along, lee.
And Tom he sat down on a stone, and he cried
Wi' Bill Brewer ...

But this isn't the end o' this shocking affair,
All along, down along, out along, lee.
Nor, though they be dead, of the horrid career
Of Bill Brewer ...

When the wind whistles cold on the moor of a night,
All along, down along, out along, lee.
Tom Pearse's old mare doth appear, gashly white,
Wi' Bill Brewer ...

And all the long night be heard skirling and groans,
All along, down along, out along, lee.
From Tom Pearse's old mare in her rattling bones,
And from Bill Brewer, Jan Stewer, Peter Gurney, Peter Davy,
Dan'l Whiddon, Harry Hawk,
Old Uncle Tom Cobley and all. *Old Uncle Tom Cobley and all.*

Traditional

What happened next?

Gradually, the Moor was opened up to the outside world as roads were given better surfaces and it became possible to drive a pony and cart both across the Moor and down to the neighbouring valleys. The Dartmoor Tin-Mining industry finally died out in the 1930s but meanwhile, with the Industrial Revolution, had come the call for thousands of pit ponies for working in coal mines throughout the country. To supply this new market, some Shetlands were introduced to try and bring down the size of the Dartmoors.

In the coal mine

On the other hand, a demand also developed nationally for a larger riding animal - good looking and free moving, but still with the stamina and good sense inherent in the little native pony. In the latter half of the nineteenth century this requirement was taken a step further when the game of polo was brought home by the Army from India, and the breeding of good native mares to cross with larger stallions to produce such ponies was actively encouraged. Indeed, in 1917 the Prince of Wales set up his own stud on Duchy of Cornwall land at Tor Royal, and for about twelve years bred partbred ponies for polo.

Polo ponies

In 1893 the Polo Pony Society had been formed for this purpose, and in 1899 Mountain and Moorland sections were opened in the Polo Pony Stud Book. Local committees were set up to produce descriptions of each native breed and, apart from a slight difference in the maximum heights allowed, the standards set up for the Dartmoor pony have not changed since. Five stallions and seventy-two mares were inspected and entered in the first Stud Book and continued to be registered in the Dartmoor Section of the National Pony Society Stud Book (as the Polo Pony Society later became) until 1979, when the Dartmoor Pony Society took over responsibility for its own registrations.

From The Maltese Cat, c. 1890

The Workers

In this electronic age, it is important to remember that we still have with us members of a generation who can recall the coming of the first motor car to their area; that milk was mainly delivered, even in London, by horse until well into the 1950s, and that although tractors were certainly used in farming before World War II, they only became universal with the development of the little grey Ferguson.

Instruction book for early Ferguson tractor, c. 1949

Even the seemingly ever-present Land-Rover was designed after 1945 when an executive of the Rover Car Company bought a surplus American jeep for his sons to have fun with; he found it so invaluable on his small Warwickshire farm that he persuaded his directors that they should improve on it for a worldwide market.

An early Land-Rover

Before the introduction of steam locomotion, horses were the universal source of motive power, but the increased mobility of the Railway Age actually added to their importance. There they were, delivering milk, bread, fish, coal, vegetables, the post. Children had to get to school, and there was shopping and visiting to be done. No one needed to be taught 'horse management', you grew up knowing what to do. Apart from the main roads the only way to cross the Moor was on foot or horseback; so it was natural that on and around Dartmoor the ponies were simply a part of everyday life.

Out riding at the beginning of this century

Princetown Fair

Moretonhampstead

Off to market

"Where be gwain?"

Down the lane

Winter

"Where's Mum?"

On the Moor

Down to Merrivale

The farms, won over the centuries from the Moor, are still much the same: small steep fields walled with the stones cleared from the land. They had to be worked by pony power, and the implements for cultivation and harvest were all pony-sized and can still be seen in museums. Where water power was not available some method had to be developed to run grain mills and other equipment; again, the pony was brought in to walk round and round inside a circular building pulling a beam attached to gears which connected with the machinery.

Typical Round House

Herding was necessary to check on the sheep and cattle grazing the open Moor, but herding of another kind was practised by the warders at Princetown Gaol escorting working parties of convicts to the quarries. For many years the prison had its own herd of Dartmoors, and part-breds were still being used by the warders until the 1970s.

Sheep being herded off the Moor

Ponies on Dartmoor

Cawsand Thunder with his mares

As far as the ponies were concerned, it must have been a good thing. With proper care, hard work never hurt anyone, and they were too important not to be looked after. By today's standards, many of them would have looked rough and maybe lean, but they were fit and hard. The herds ran from their owners' farms, and although the breeding programmes may *seem* to have been a haphazard affair they were certainly not, and the better strains of both male and female bloodlines were jealously guarded and prized. No matter that early records state an individual pony's parentage as being simply 'Dartmoor pony' on both sides - generally speaking, someone knew how it was bred. They simply had not had time to write it down - anyway, why worry? They were good stock doing the job they were needed for.

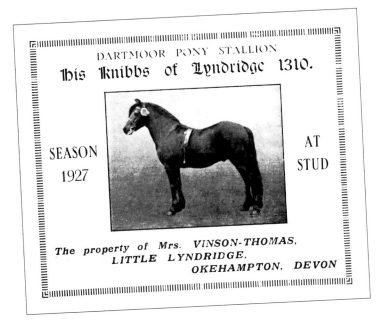

His Knibbs' stud card

A Changing World

But times were changing after World War II, though slowly at first with the postwar austerity. Electricity finally arrived on most of the farms, mechanisation transformed agriculture, life got easier for everyone and suddenly the ponies were redundant. However, it didn't seem to matter - the Moor was there for them as before.

With time again for leisure, all over the country people took up riding - pony-mad little girls became very common and the horse and pony boom of the Sixties and early Seventies had arrived. Now the characteristics that had made the ponies such good workers totally fitted the bill for modern childrens' ponies. People with Dartmoor roots now living elsewhere picked up the threads of their old lives, breeding from the old family herds and passing on their enthusiasm to others. Newcomers moved into the Dartmoor area and joined the locals in setting up their own studs, learning about the history and ancestry of the breed and carrying on the famous lines.

It was different though: no longer the working animal, these ponies were often prized simply for their beauty, and did their new job superlatively well. For a time it seemed that the best ponies were leaving the Moor for the bright lights of the show and competition worlds. Exports became a feature; most European countries do not have our great wealth of native ponies for their children to ride and France, the Netherlands, Scandinavia and West Germany showed interest and bought significant numbers to set up their own Breed Societies, later followed by Australia and the United States.

Many of the Dartmoor farmers must have felt that their ponies were being taken over by the rest of the world. The newcomers seemed tremendously keen on what they were doing and learning all they could, but it was not what they were used to. Gleaming ponies, cossetted, rugged and exquisitely presented arrived at all the shows, brought by strangers not really aware of Dartmoor traditions. As well as carrying off many prizes, they transformed the scene. Luckily for the future, some farmers joined in, took on the newcomers at their new game and held their own. However, many simply let them get on with it.

The ponies still ran on the Moor, but gradually breeding plans lapsed. Farms were sold and new people moved in, taking over the Commoners' Rights. Ignorant of the awesome conditions, they turned out animals that lacked the hardiness needed to withstand the cruel winters. Sadly, these ponies were not only endangered themselves, but by mixing with the indigenous herds they produced progeny who were diluting the stock.

Winter on the Moor

It seemed that there were two breeds of Dartmoor ponies: the lovely stud-bred family and show ponies, and the apparently unloved and uncared-for herds on the Moor, breeding more or less haphazardly and producing weaker animals.

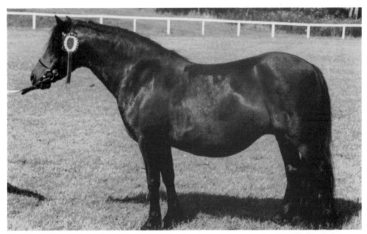

Hisley Polonaise

Wintering out

The Annual Drifts continued, with more and more of the foals going straight to the pet-food trade. With hindsight, who can say that was so dreadful · at least it was a quick end. Horror stories hit the headlines: starving ponies, helicopter drops of hay by welfare organisations, prosecutions and so on. It was a bad period, and things seemed to have got out of control.

Flydon Tor Royal, owned and driven by Mrs V. Parkinson

Who are you?

On the Newtake

The Moorland Schemes

Finally it was agreed that something had to be done. A group of interested people from the Dartmoor Pony Society, the Duchy of Cornwall (which owns most of the Moor), the National Park Authority and the Ministry of Agriculture got together and the Dartmoor Moorland Scheme was born.

The plan was to encourage owners to breed selectively again and to register their ponies, to foster interest in the enormous heritage going to waste and to try and improve the condition of all the ponies on the Moor. It had to be a long-term plan - the only alternative was to take everything off the Moor and start again, which would be impossible.

In 1988 the first Newtake (a local name for a fenced area of Moor) was set up at Brownberry, near Two Bridges.

Building a drystone wall

Dunnabridge Newtake

The Committee selected a stallion, approved for his breeding, type and hardiness. Farmers with mares of good Dartmoor type, but with no record of breeding, were invited to submit them for inspection. If accepted, these mares were recorded in a new Supplementary Register and in the first year twenty mares entered the Scheme and ran in the Newtake with the stallion all the summer. The following year another Newtake at Huccaby was used, and two herds of seventeen mares each ran with their stallions. To give the foals a better start, in the autumn they were weaned and wintered off the Moor on land provided by the National Trust.

Interest was rising, and the addition of another Newtake at Dunnabridge means that there are now three herds out every summer with different stallions, ensuring a good spread of bloodlines. Each autumn the ponies are gathered for return to their owners' herds, the foals inspected, ear-tagged and their markings recorded to identify them in the register. The quality of the foals is improving each year and many of the mares return every spring, so satisfied are their owners. Soon fillies born in the Newtakes will be old enough to return themselves, to take the Scheme on a stage further.

At the same time, seeing the success of the Moorland Scheme, the Dartmoor Commoners' Council and the National Park Authority decided to try and improve the overall standard of the rest of the ponies on the Moor. In 1989, owners were invited to submit their herds for inspection by a Dartmoor breeder, and a member and a vet from the Dartmoor Commoners' Council. This again is a serious assessment of type and condition, with no 'rubber stamp' pass. Plenty fail, but those accepted receive grants for up to twenty mares, one adult stallion and one colt. Inspection takes place in January, when conditions are at their bleakest and the ponies must be in acceptable condition to prosper through the rest of the winter.

The two schemes running in parallel mean that some of the better colts from the Newtakes come back to the National Park scheme to improve the progeny of the still-unregistered mares. Each year the numbers of ponies coming forward for grants has increased, as has that of those accepted, and the general overall interest in the ponies is increasing.

Guided walks are organised by the National Park Authority during the summer so that visitors can see the ponies running in the Newtakes, and each September a Moorland Show is held at Princetown on Carnival Day when the stud and Moor breeders and owners come together to compete with each other in the different classes (including one for mares from the Schemes). The latter now hold their own in this company.

Princetown Fair

So, what of the future?

No one can ever be sure. Certainly the two Moorland Schemes are running well, improving the standard and continuing to attract new owners and supporters each year. The locals and the outsiders find that their interests blend and that each has something to contribute to the other, so that more and more they are becoming simply Dartmoor pony breeders and owners, whether they live in Devon, Scotland or France. The future value of the gene-bank of old bloodlines to the modern breeders, combined with the realisation that better-presented ponies command better prices, has forged a good bridge between the two types of enthusiasts that must augur well for the ponies' future.

Strict European Community regulations on abattoirs have seen the virtual end of the meat market, certainly for small foals, in spite of protestations to the contrary from some emotional pressure groups. A present worry, in fact, is the fate of loads of assorted foals bought at sales and shipped up-country to be sold as 'saved from slaughter'.

Wendel Sweet William, ridden by Katy Tyler, competing in the National Pony Society's Mountain and Moorland Working Hunter Pony Championships at the Horse of the Year Show 1992, where he was placed 3rd.

In the modern competitive horse world, the Dartmoor holds its own and regularly beats the best the country can produce in virtually all disciplines. As well as being used as an ideal mount for children, lightweight adults have discovered that what suited the herding farmers fifty years ago can also do the same for them today.

Head held high, mane and tail flying, the Dartmoor looks to the twenty-first century with pride and confidence.

Wendel Sea Dragon

The Dartmoor National Park Authority

The ponies of Dartmoor

Government subsidies are available for farmers grazing sheep and cattle on the moor but there are no Government subsidies for keeping ponies. This is one reason for the decline in the number of ponies on the moor. Ponies are no longer needed as working farm animals - another reason for their decline. In 1950 there were 30,000 ponies on the moor, today there are fewer than 3,000.

Two schemes have been set up to aid the survival of the ponies and to encourage the breeding of pure Dartmoors.

Dartmoor Pony Support Scheme

This scheme was set up by the Dartmoor National Park Authority with advice from the Dartmoor Commoners' Council. It was introduced in October 1988, for a trial period of three years, extended to six years. Under the scheme, ponykeepers may apply for support payment if their herds are living and breeding on the commons and if their mares conform to an agreed definition of the Dartmoor type. Inspections are made by experts each year to ensure that the conditions of the scheme are complied with and payments are made for a maximum of twenty mares per holding + 1 adult and 1 young stallion. In 1992, 63 farmers were supported with payments for 827 mares, 41 adult stallions and 19 young stallions. The scheme has succeeded in arresting decline in numbers of ponies, and has led to better selection of drift time for a more improved type.

Dartmoor Pony Moorland Scheme

This scheme is administered by the Duchy of Cornwall and supported by the Dartmoor Pony Society and the Dartmoor National Park Authority. The main aim is to encourage moorland farmers to return to breeding pure Dartmoors. It will also re-establish a fresh gene pool of use to breeders all over the country.

In Spring 1988 a breeding programme was introduced for a trial period of three years. A group of 20 approved moorland mares was kept with a fully registered Dartmoor stallion at Brownberry Newtake near Dunnabridge during the breeding season (May to September) after which the mares were returned to their owners to graze on the open moor and foal in the spring.

The scheme has now extended to nearby Huccaby and Dunnabridge Newtakes and 45 mares are involved.

Several guided walks take place to the ponies in Dunnabridge.

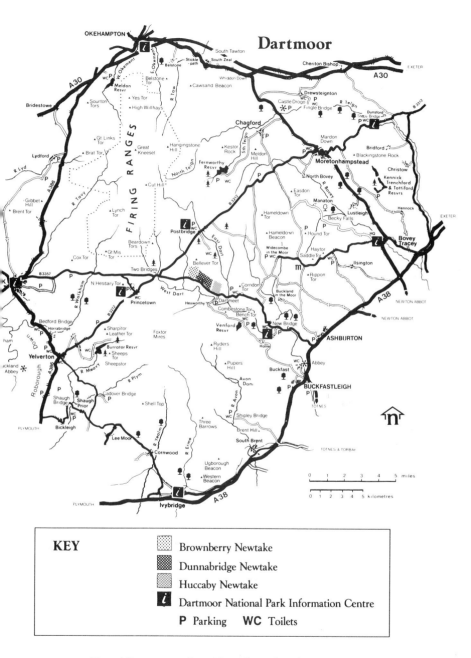

Dartmoor

KEY	
▦	Brownberry Newtake
▦	Dunnabridge Newtake
▦	Huccaby Newtake
i	Dartmoor National Park Information Centre
P Parking	**WC** Toilets

No public access to these Newtakes other than via
Dartmoor National Park guided walks. See page 35.

The Standard of the Dartmoor Pony

Height: Not exceeding 12.2hh.

Colour: Bay, brown, black, grey, chestnut, roan. Piebalds & skewbalds are not allowed. Excessive white markings should be discouraged.

Head: Should be small, well set on and bloodlike, with the nostrils large and expanding, and the eyes bright, mild, intelligent and prominent. The ears should be small, well-formed, alert and neatly set. The throat and jaws should be fine and showing no signs of coarsenes or throatiness.

Neck: Strong, but not too heavy, and of medium length. Stallions have a moderate crest.

Shoulders: Good shoulders are most important. They should be well laid back and sloping, but not too fine at the withers.

Body: Of medium length and strong, well ribbed up and with a good depth of girth giving plenty of heart room.

Loin and Hindquarters: Strong and well covered with muscle. The hindquarters should be of medium length and neither level nor steeply sloping. The tail is well set up.

Hind Legs: The hocks should be well let down with plenty of length from hip to hock, clean cut and with plenty of bone below the joint. They should not be "sickled" or "cow-hocked".

Fore Legs: Should not be tied in, in any way, at the elbows. The fore-arm should be muscular and the knee fairly large and flat on the front. The cannon should be short from knee to fetlock with ample, good, flat, flinty bone. The pasterns should be sloping but not too long. The feet should be sound, tough and well shaped.

Movement: Low straight and free-flowing, yet without exaggeration.

General: The mane and tail should be full and flowing. The Dartmoor is a very good looking riding pony, sturdily built yet with quality.

Further information is available from:
Dartmoor Pony Society Honorary Secretary
Mrs L. Setter
Puddaven Farm · North Bovey · Newton Abbot · Devon TQ13 8RF